Published by SL Resources, Inc.
A Division of Student Life

Student Life
Attn: Ministry Resources
2183 Parkway Lake Drive
Birmingham, AL 35226

Unless otherwise indicated, all Scripture quotations are taken from the Holy Bible: New International Version (North American Edition), copyright ©1973, 1978, 1984, by International Bible Society. Used by permission of Zondervan Publishing House.

ISBN-10: 1-935040-79-0
ISBN-13: 978-1-935040-79-8

31 Verses Every Teenager Should Know™

www.studentlife.com
www.31verses.com

Printed in the United States of America

31 verses

EVERY TEENAGER
SHOULD KNOW

So, just what is this "Re" thing all about?

Simply put, it's about the requirements of the Christian life. These are requirements like the ones found in Micah 6:1-8 where God basically reveals that what He requires is that His people reflect His character in response to His faithfulness.

Did you catch that? There were four "Re" words right there, and that's just skimming the surface.

Repent. Relate. Remain. Reach. Receive. Resolve. Resign. Rest. Restore. Retain. Represent. Retreat. Return. Reward. Redeem. Reform. Rejoice. Regard. Reply. Reveal. Request. Rebuke. Rely. Rescue. Reason. Rebuff. Remember. Revive. Renew.

These are all examples of God's requirements for our lives. However, they're not a bunch of regulations designed to keep us in line and make sure we earn God's approval. They're extensions of the reality of our relationship with Him, results of our being reconciled to Him through our faith in Jesus Christ.

If it's still a little confusing for you, then don't worry about it. Take each devotion one day at a time. Prayerfully seek what God has to say to you through His Word about the grand journey with Him to which He is calling you.

All this book is really trying to answer is this: Once we choose to follow God, what exactly does He expect out of us? There's much more than we can cover here, but it's a start.

I won't promise you that we've got all the answers to all your questions, but I do want you to know that we've been right where you are and we've made it so far. We believe in you and know that you can do it too. Thanks for letting us join you on your journey with Jesus Christ for just a while.

Regards,

Chris Kinsely

Now that you own this incredible little book, you may be wondering, "What do I do with it?"

Glad you asked . . . The great thing about this book is that you can use it just about any way you want.

It's not a system. It's a resource that can be used in ways that are as unique and varied as you are.

A few suggestions . . .

THE "ONE MONTH" PLAN

On this plan, you'll read one devotional each day for a month. This is a great way to immerse yourself in the Bible for a month-long period. (OK, we realize that every month doesn't have 31 days. But 28 or 30 is close enough to 31, right?) The idea is to cover a lot of information in a short amount of time.

THE "SCRIPTURE MEMORY" PLAN

The idea behind this plan is to memorize the verse for each day's devotional; you don't move on to the next devotional until you have memorized the one you're on. If you're like most people, this might take you more than one day per devotional. So, this plan takes a slower approach.

THE "I'M NO WILLIAM SHAKESPEARE" PLAN

Don't like to write or journal? This plan is for you . . . Listen, not everyone expresses themselves the same. If you don't like to express yourself through writing, that's OK. Simply read the devotional for each verse, then read the questions. Think about them. Pray through them. But don't feel like you have to journal if you don't want to.

THE "STRENGTH IN NUMBERS" PLAN

God designed humans for interaction. We are social creatures. How cool would it be if you could go through "31:Re" with your friends? Get a group of friends together. Consider agreeing to read five verses each week, then meeting to talk about it.

Pretty simple, right? Choose a plan. Or make up your own. But get started already. What are you waiting on?

REQUIRE

MICAH 6:8

He has showed you, O man, what is good. And what does the LORD require of you? To act justly and to love mercy and to walk humbly with your God.

HAVE YOU EVER BEEN IN A SITUATION LIKE THIS BEFORE? YOU HAVE A FRIEND WITH WHOM YOU ARE REALLY CLOSE, BUT FOR SOME REASON LATELY THEY'VE SEEMED PRETTY DISTANT. THEY'RE NOT RETURNING YOUR TEXTS. THEY PRETENDED NOT TO HEAR YOU WHEN YOU WERE YELLING AT THEM ACROSS THE PARKING LOT, AND YOU'VE GOT THE SNEAKING SUSPICION THAT THEY'VE BEEN AVOIDING YOU IN THE HALLWAY. FINALLY, THEY COME TO YOU AND ASK YOU WHAT THEY'VE DONE TO MAKE YOU TREAT THEM LIKE YOU DO.

YOU'RE CAUGHT COMPLETELY OFF GUARD. AFTER THE TWO OF YOU TALK ABOUT IT YOU REALIZE THAT SOME FLIPPANT COMMENT YOU MADE THAT YOU MEANT AS A JOKE REALLY HURT THEM. NOW THAT YOU KNOW, ALL YOU WANT TO DO IS MAKE IT UP TO THEM. THE ONLY PROBLEM IS, YOU DON'T REALLY KNOW HOW.

READ MICAH 6:1-8.

THROUGH THE PROPHET MICAH GOD MADE IT CLEAR THAT HE WAS NOT HAPPY WITH THE PEOPLE OF ISRAEL. HE HAD BEEN COMPLETELY FAITHFUL TO THEM, YET THEY CONTINUOUSLY IGNORED ALL HE HAD DONE AND TURNED AWAY FROM HIM. ONCE HE REMINDED THEM THE PEOPLE RESPONDED BY QUESTIONING WHAT IT WOULD TAKE TO PLEASE GOD. THEY WILDLY WONDERED WHAT EXTREMES TO WHICH HE WOULD MAKE THEM GO IN ORDER TO BE RESTORED IN THEIR RELATIONSHIP WITH HIM.

HOWEVER, GOD HAD MADE IT CLEAR THAT HE HAD NEVER LEFT THEM, AND HAD ALREADY LET THEM KNOW WHAT HE REQUIRED OF THEM IN RESPONSE TO HIS FAITHFULNESS. DO WHAT'S RIGHT AND FAIR. SHOW SELFLESS COMPASSION TOWARDS OTHERS. LIVE IN UNION WITH GOD AS LORD.

WE OFTEN RESPOND TO GOD'S FAITHFULNESS IN THE SAME WAS AS THE PEOPLE OF ISRAEL, BY FORGETTING. WHEN WE REMEMBER, THOUGH, WE CAN KNOW THAT WHAT HE REQUIRES OF US IS THE SAME AS THEM TOO.

1. What does it mean to "act justly?"

2. In what ways does mercy define the way we are to love others?

3. How can we demonstrate humility in our walk with God?

4. Write a prayer to God below to thank Him for making His requirements for us very clear. Recognize that these requirements don't earn His favor but are done in response to it. Commit to fulfill these requirements today.

ROMANS 8:31

What, then, shall we say in response to this? If God is for us, who can be against us?

Maryam and Marzieh are two Iranian women who grew up in Muslim families. In their late 20s, Maryam and Marzieh were arrested and placed in one of the world's worst jails for being "anti-government." In other words, the Iranian government found out that these two women had turned from Islam and were now Christ-followers.

Throughout their time in prison, Maryam's health and Marzieh's health both suffered tremendously; untreated infections, headaches, fever, and severe back pain all plagued them. When brought before a judge and ordered to recant their faith in Christ, Maryam and Marzieh refused. Although they knew that this would result in continued persecution, they knew that no amount of pain or persecution could ever compete with their hope in the promise of eternity with Christ. By the grace of God, after 259 days in prison, Maryam and Marzieh were set free. Though many praised their faithfulness, the two women responded by acknowledging that the deliverance had nothing to do with them but everything to do with God.

Read Romans 8:31–39.

"If God is for us, who can be against us?" This is the attitude that Paul keeps in the face of persecution. He knows that despite all suffering and trial and hardship that he faces, he can overcome it all because he is a follower of Christ, a conqueror through Christ. Paul goes on to say that he is sure that absolutely nothing can separate believers from the love of Christ—not even death itself. Despite all that he goes through, Paul continues to find hope and strength to endure through this promise.

All Christ-followers experience trouble in one form or another. It is often in these moments, whenever living for God ceases to be easy, that the world looks closely at us to see how we respond. So the question for you is: How will you respond?

1. WHAT STORIES DO YOU KNOW OF PEOPLE WHO HAVE ENCOUNTERED SOME KIND OF TROUBLE FOR THEIR FAITH?

2. IN WHAT WAYS HAVE YOU EXPERIENCED TROUBLE BECAUSE YOU'VE CHOSEN TO FOLLOW JESUS CHRIST?

3. HOW DOES GOD BEING "FOR" YOU AFFECT HOW YOU RESPOND WHENEVER YOU ENCOUNTER TROUBLE?

4. WRITE A PRAYER BELOW TO GOD AND CONFESS YOUR RELIANCE ON HIS PRESENCE IN YOUR LIFE. THANK HIM FOR ALWAYS BEING FOR YOU. SEEK HIS HELP IN KNOWING HOW TO RESPOND TO WHATEVER LIFE MIGHT THROW YOUR WAY, WHETHER GOOD OR BAD.

Repent, then, and turn to God, so that your sins may be wiped out, that times of refreshing may come from the Lord . . .

VERSE

three

repent

IF YOU HAVE COME CLOSE TO A RADIO IN THE LAST 20 YEARS, THEN YOU HAVE MOST LIKELY HEARD THE SONG "TOTAL ECLIPSE OF THE HEART" BY BONNIE TYLER. IT IS ONE OF THE MOST POPULAR SONGS OF ALL TIME AND HAS LATELY BECOME A TRENDY CHOICE IN MANY A CHURCH'S DRAMATIC PRESENTATION. SOMETIMES SUCH DRAMAS CAN BE A LITTLE CHEESY, BUT THEY DO PLAY UPON A TUNE THAT IS FAMILIAR TO MOST PEOPLE. THE SONG WAS RELEASED IN 1983 AND HAS SOLD MORE THAN 60 MILLION COPIES IN ALMOST 30 YEARS. AT ONE TIME, "TOTAL ECLIPSE OF THE HEART" WAS SELLING MORE THAN 60,000 COPIES A DAY AS THE TOP SONG IN THE UNITED STATES.

THOUGH IT WILL FOREVER BE ENSHRINED AS A CATCHY TUNE, "TOTAL ECLIPSE OF THE HEART" ALSO SEEMS TO IMPART SOME UNINTENDED SPIRITUAL INSIGHT. MANY VERSES IN THE SONG BEGIN WITH "TURNAROUND." THE REPEATED USE OF THIS PHRASE HELPS TO DEFINE A BIBLICAL WORD THAT MEANS A GREAT DEAL TO A BELIEVER'S WALK WITH CHRIST.

READ ACTS 3:17—20.

THE WORD REPENT LITERALLY MEANS "TURN AROUND" OR "TURN BACK." IN OTHER WORDS, WE SHOULD TURN BACK TOWARD GOD AND TURN AWAY FROM OUR SIN. THIS VERSE IN PARTICULAR CHALLENGES US TO TURN AROUND FROM OUR WICKED WAYS AND WALK TOWARD CHRIST, WHO FORGIVES SIN AND REFRESHES THE SOUL. TO REPENT IS TO TURN AWAY FROM ALL SELFISHNESS AND ALL UNGODLY DESIRES AND HABITS IN FAVOR OF TAKING ON ALL OF CHRIST.

WHAT AREAS IN YOUR LIFE DO YOU NEED TO TURN AWAY FROM IN ORDER TO WALK TOWARD CHRIST? TRUE JOY IS FOUND IN CHRIST AND CHRIST ALONE, AND WHEN YOU RESPOND IN REPENTANCE TO THAT TRUTH, YOU WILL FIND TRUE SATISFACTION AND A GREAT TIME OF REFRESHMENT IN YOUR SOUL.

1. What are some of the things you have to do in life that you really wish you didn't?

2. How does striving to work as if you're working for God change the way you approach jobs, chores and responsibilities you have?

3. What is the reward that God promises us?

4. Write a prayer to God below thanking Him for His promised reward. Seek His strength and discipline to work through whatever life brings you as though you are working for Him.

Psalm 33:8

Let all the earth fear the LORD; let all the people of the world revere him.

What does it mean to revere something? Not sure? Well, okay, let's try another word . . . What does it mean to adore something? There are actually several meanings of this word. To adore something can refer to liking it very much, possessing a strong admiration or utmost respect for it, or even worshipping it. Think about people, places, and memories that you adore. When we truly adore something, when we revere it, we hold it in such high esteem that it can potentially become the focus and driving force of life.

Read Psalm 33:1–9.

Verse 8 lies in the middle of three verses recounting the story of Creation, in which whatever God spoke and commanded came into being right then and there. That is truly awesome power! He created the seas and basically told them where to stop. He looks at mountains and makes them tremble. He knows the number of stars in the sky and grains of sand on the ground. He created every creature on the planet. All fear, reverence, and devotion belong to Him for all of these reasons and many, many more.

How many times have you looked into the face of God and said, "No thanks"? That's a scary question, isn't it? But we human beings do this all the time. We look at God, the Creator of the universe and all that is in it, and say, "I know that you created me and all, but I think I can handle this one better on my own." Stop and think about that response—it sounds pretty crazy, huh? Think once again about the different people, places, memories, and other things that you adore. Now consider this: Every single thing that you thought of was created by God. Since this is true, all of creation, including you, should humbly stand in awe and adoration of the Creator. That's what it's like to revere Him.

]REFLECT

1. Describe what it means to revere something.

2. In what ways do you revere God?

3. What hinders you from revering God?

4. Write a prayer to God below and express your awesome adoration of Him for all that He has done and for all that He is. Commit to revering Him to the point that He is the top priority in your life and serves as the sole focus and motivation for everything that you do, think, and say.

REGARD

1 THESSALONIANS 5:13

Hold them in the highest regard in love because of their work. Live in peace with each other.

EVERY SPORTS FAN KNOWS THAT BEHIND EVERY GREAT TEAM IS A GREAT COACH. THIS IS ESPECIALLY TRUE FOR SOME OF THE MOST SUCCESSFUL COLLEGE FOOTBALL TEAMS OVER THE YEARS. YOU MAY BE THINKING OF SCHOOLS LIKE NOTRE DAME, OKLAHOMA, LSU, MICHIGAN, SOUTHERN CAL, FLORIDA, AUBURN, AND SO ON. EACH OF THESE SCHOOLS IS KNOWN FOR HAVING A WINNING TRADITION, WHICH THEY ULTIMATELY OWE TO THE COACH WHO LED THEM TO VICTORY. IT IS COMMON FOR THESE SCHOOLS TO CELEBRATE A GREAT COACH AND THE WINNING TRADITION THAT WAS A PRODUCT OF HIS LEADERSHIP.

WHAT MAKES A GREAT COACH IS HOW HE IS ABLE TO CHALLENGE HIS PLAYERS TO PUSH THEMSELVES TO GIVE AN EXCELLENT PERFORMANCE EVEN WHEN IT IS DIFFICULT. THE MARK OF A GOOD COACH IS FINDING A WAY TO SAY HARD THINGS TO PLAYERS IN A WAY THAT MOTIVATES THEM TO PERFORM BETTER THAN THEY EVER THOUGHT THEY COULD. THIS EVENTUALLY LEADS THE PLAYERS TO REGARD THE COACH WITH GREAT AND LASTING RESPECT.

READ 1 THESSALONIANS 5:12—15.

THERE WERE SOME PEOPLE IN THE CHURCH AT THESSALONICA WHO WERE NOT RECEIVING INSTRUCTION FROM THE LEADERS IN THE CHURCH AS THEY WERE SUPPOSED TO, AND THEY WERE REGARDING THE LEADERS WITH DISDAIN INSTEAD OF TRUST. PAUL NOW WRITES TO THEM TO TELL THEM THAT THEY NEED TO REGARD THEIR LEADERS WITH LOVE INSTEAD OF RIDICULE.

GOD PUTS SPIRITUAL LEADERS IN OUR LIVES TO HELP US GROW CLOSER TO HIM. JUST AS A COACH CHALLENGES YOU TO BE BETTER AT A SPORT, THE LEADERSHIP OF YOUR CHURCH EXISTS TO CHALLENGE YOU IN YOUR WALK WITH CHRIST. IT IS UP TO YOU TO DECIDE IF YOU WILL RECEIVE CORRECTION FROM YOUR LEADERS OR REBEL AGAINST IT. YOUR ABILITY TO RECEIVE CORRECTION FROM THOSE WHO ARE MORE MATURE IN THE FAITH WILL DEFINE WHAT YOUR WALK WITH CHRIST LOOKS LIKE.

1. Who are some leaders that God has placed in your life to challenge and instruct you in spiritual matters?

2. How do you currently submit to or rebel against their leadership?

3. Why is it often difficult for you to receive correction or instruction?

4. Write a prayer to God below and thank Him for the leaders that He has placed in your life. Ask for His help in gracefully receiving and responding to their instruction and correction. Commit to regarding them with the love and respect that is due them in accordance with God's Word.

EPHESIANS 5:11

Have nothing to do with the fruitless deeds of darkness, but rather expose them.

Were you ever afraid of the dark when you were a kid? It's okay—you can admit it. So many of us were. After all, everything is so much more mysterious and scarier in the dark.

In the dark, your imagination runs wild and convinces you that there must be terrible things lurking under your bed and around the corner. The darkness plays tricks on you and casts unidentifiable shadows that convince you that the boogeyman is just waiting to snatch you up. Yet with just one flip of a light switch, that monster or creature that you were convinced was about to get you is amazingly revealed to be just a harmless pillow or a chair.

Read Ephesians 5:6–10.

Unfortunately, we live in a world that is filled with spiritual darkness. We may often feel that scary and menacing forces are lurking close to our lives. These forces, when left alone, can threaten to tear our lives apart. In these verses, the apostle Paul tells us to not be partners with the sons of disobedience: "For at one time you were darkness, but now you are light in the Lord. Live as children of light."

Paul gives us examples of what our lives should look like if we are truly walking in the light of Christ. When we have a relationship with Christ, the dark places in our lives should be illuminated. As Christians, we should be a light to others that leads them to the greatness and holiness of who Jesus is. We should also bring light to those who are suffering in the darkness. As we live in the midst of darkness, let's strive to illuminate many lives, including our own, with the light of God's Word each and every day.

1. WHY DO YOU THINK THAT DARKNESS IS SOMETHING SO WIDELY CONSIDERED AS FRIGHTENING?

2. IN WHAT WAYS ARE YOU BEING A LIGHT TO OTHERS IN A SPIRITUALLY DARK WORLD?

3. WHAT AREAS IN YOUR LIFE NEED TO BE ILLUMINATED?

4. WRITE A PRAYER TO GOD BELOW AND SEEK HIS ASSISTANCE IN ILLUMINATING ANY DARK PLACES IN YOUR LIFE. COMMIT TO WALKING AS A "CHILD OF LIGHT." ASK HIM TO EMPOWER YOU TO BE A BEACON OF LIGHT TO PEOPLE AROUND YOU.

Luke 17:3

*"So watch yourselves. If your brother sins, rebuke
him, and if he repents, forgive him."*

VERSE

fifteen
rebuke

ONE OF THE GREATEST BLESSINGS OF FOLLOWING JESUS IS
THAT WE ARE NOT LEFT TO GO IT ALONE. THE NEW TESTA-
MENT PICTURE OF FOLLOWING JESUS IS NOT THAT OF IRON
MAN SINGLEHANDEDLY TAKING ON ALL THE EVILS OF THE
WORLD.

RATHER, THE HOLY SPIRIT ACTS AS OUR GUIDE AND COM-
FORTER AS WE FOLLOW JESUS. ADDITIONALLY, WE FOLLOW
JESUS AS PART OF A COMMUNITY. THIS COMMUNITY PRO-
VIDES US WITH FRIENDSHIP, SUPPORT, AND ACCOUNTABIL-
ITY. COMMUNITY ALLOWS US TO SHARE OUR STRUGGLES
AND HELPS US TO GUARD AGAINST TEMPTATION. COMMU-
NITY SAYS, "WE ARE HERE TO HELP YOU TO BE MORE LIKE
JESUS."

READ LUKE 17:1—4.

HERE, JESUS IS TEACHING HIS FOLLOWERS ABOUT HOW TO
GUARD AGAINST THE TEMPTATION TO SIN. THE WARNING IS
NOT JUST TO AVOID SIN BUT ALSO TO NOT CAUSE SOMEONE
ELSE TO SIN. JESUS' LANGUAGE HERE IS STRONG. IN VERSE
TWO HE CLAIMS THAT IT WOULD BE BETTER FOR A MAN TO
HAVE A HEAVY ROCK TIED AROUND HIS NECK AND THROWN
IN THE SEA THAN TO CAUSE SOMEONE ELSE TO SIN. HE WAS
PRETTY SERIOUS ABOUT IT. WE SHOULD BE TOO.

VERSE THREE CONTAINS THREE COMMANDS THAT ARE RE-
LATED TO SIN AND COMMUNITY. THE FIRST IS TO PAY AT-
TENTION TO OURSELVES. WE MUST FIRST MAKE SURE THAT
WE DO NOT FALL INTO SIN. SECOND, IF WE SEE ANOTHER
BELIEVER ENGAGED IN SIN, WE ARE TO REBUKE HIM OR
HER. WE SHOULD CORRECT SOMEONE ELSE OUT OF LOVE
AND NOT OUT OF A DESIRE TO MAKE OURSELVES APPEAR
MORE HOLY OR MATURE IN THE FAITH. THIS ALSO MEANS
THAT WE MUST ALLOW OURSELVES TO BE REBUKED WHEN-
EVER WE SIN. THIRD, JESUS COMMANDS US TO FORGIVE
SOMEONE WHO REPENTS OF HIS OR HER SIN. THE GOAL IS
TO RESTORE THE RELATIONSHIP. WE DON'T HOLD THE SIN
OVER THE PERSON'S HEAD BUT RATHER MERCIFULLY WEL-
COME HIM OR HER BACK INTO THE FELLOWSHIP OF BE-
LIEVERS. THAT IS COMMUNITY.

REJOICE
REGARD
REPLY
REVEAL
REQUEST
REBUKE
REFLECT
RELY
RESCUE
REASON
REBUFF
REMEMBER
REVIVE
REACH
RECEIVE
RESOLVE
RESIGN
RESTORE
RETAIN
REPRESENT
RETREAT
RETURN

1. How can I make sure that I am not causing other people to sin?

2. In what ways has my Christian community helped me to keep from sinning?

3. In what ways has my Christian community helped to restore me when I have sinned?

4. Write a prayer to God below and thank Him for the community with which He has surrounded you. Ask Him to help you fulfill the commands that He has given you concerning sin in your community. Repent of your sins and seek to be used to help restore others in your community.

---

1 John 4:16
And so we know and rely on the love God has for us. God is love. Whoever lives in love lives in God, and God in him.

If you've ever been bungee jumping, you've gained some valuable experience in reliance. After all, this is an activity that is basically crazy to begin with. You climb up to some ridiculous height. You attach yourself to a relatively thin cord that is basically an overgrown rubber band. Then you jump. You hurl towards the ground below you at a speed that would normally result in a pretty major injury at the very least, and trust that the tension of the out-stretched line will stop you and bounce you back up.

Of course, there are any number of factors in this scenario that could go wrong and fail, which would result in a pretty bad day for everyone involved. Still, an untold number of people every year decide that their particular band of rubber strings is trustworthy and something on which they can fully rely.

Read 1 John 4:15-18.

In our darkest and scariest and most confusing moments of life we can find ourselves questioning God. That's the honest truth, isn't it? We begin to wonder if what we believe is really true. We ask ourselves if God really is who He says He is. We ponder whether or not He can be trusted or whether or not we're someone about whom He can really care. In those moments we are often left wondering what we can hold on to or what will hold on to us.

The answer, of course, is God's love. We can look back through Scripture and history and discover that God has always been faithful. He has always kept His Word. He has always proved to be whom He claimed. He has always come through for His people for one reason: He loves them. He loves you, and on that you most certainly can rely.

]REFLECT

1. What are some current fears, worries or troubles that you're facing?

_____

2. What kind of questions about God do difficult periods of life sometimes cause you to ask?

_____

3. How can you know that you can fully rely on God's love for you?

_____

4. Write a prayer to God below thanking Him for His love on which you can fully rely. Confess any doubts, questions, concerns or fears you might have and ask Him to relieve them. Commit to continue to rely on the love He has for you.

_____

REASON

1 PETER 3:15

But in your hearts set apart Christ as Lord. Always be prepared to give an answer to everyone who asks you to give the reason for the hope that you have. But do this with gentleness and respect . . .

HAVE YOU EVER NOTICED THAT CHILDREN GO THROUGH PHASES IN WHICH THEY ASK LOTS OF QUESTIONS? "WHAT'S THAT?" "WHO'S THAT?" "ARE WE THERE YET?" "WHY? WHY? WHY?" I REMEMBER GOING THROUGH THIS PHASE WHEN I WAS A CHILD. DO YOU?

WHAT I REMEMBER MOST ABOUT THIS PHASE WAS HOW FRUSTRATED I WOULD BECOME WHENEVER MY PARENTS ANSWERED MY QUESTIONS WITH JUST ONE WORD, THE ONE WORD THAT DOESN'T CUT IT AS A REAL ANSWER: "BECAUSE." ASKING A QUESTION SHOWS THAT YOU ARE CURIOUS ABOUT SOMETHING AND IMPLIES THAT YOU WANT A THOROUGH EXPLANATION. YOU WANT A GOOD REASON FOR WHY SOMETHING IS HAPPENING, WHAT SOMETHING IS, OR HOW SOMETHING CAN BE POSSIBLE. YOU WANT WHOEVER YOU ARE ASKING THE QUESTION TO BE READY TO ANSWER WITH THAT REASON.

READ 1 PETER 3:13—17.

PETER IS WRITING TO CHRISTIANS IN THE EARLY CHURCH WHO ARE IN THE MIDST OF SUFFERING DUE TO THEIR FAITH IN CHRIST. NONBELIEVERS HAD NOTICED THAT THESE PEOPLE LIVED DIFFERENTLY, WHICH PROVOKED MANY QUESTIONS AS TO WHY THAT WAS THE CASE. IN ORDER TO BE ABLE TO ANSWER THE QUESTIONS OF NONBELIEVERS AND DEFEND THEIR FAITH, PETER URGES CHRISTIANS TO ALWAYS BE PREPARED WITH A REASON FOR WHY THEY FIND THEIR HOPE IN JESUS CHRIST. HE EMPHASIZES AT THE END OF THIS VERSE TO COAT THEIR REASON WITH GENTLENESS AND RESPECT SO AS TO MOST EFFECTIVELY REACH THOSE WITH WHOM THEY ARE SHARING THEIR FAITH.

THE SAME IS TRUE FOR US TODAY. WE NEED TO TAKE TIME TO THINK THROUGH THE REASON THAT WE HAVE FOR OUR FAITH. WE NEED TO BE READY TO PROVIDE AN ANSWER TO ANYONE WHO QUESTIONS US. THIS TAKES GREAT EFFORT. AFTER ALL, "BECAUSE" JUST WON'T CUT IT.

1. What questions about your faith have you been asked before?

2. How prepared do you feel to answer questions about your faith?

3. Write out the reason for why you have chosen to place your faith in Jesus Christ.

4. Write a prayer to God below and share with Him some of the questions that you have been asked before. Seek His assistance in preparing you to be able to answer any questions. Thank Him for being reason enough to live as a good example to everyone around you.

PSALM 105:5
Remember the wonders he has done, his miracles, and the judgments he pronounced...

Have you ever watched the Academy Awards? There is a whole lot of hoopla that goes along with this very prestigious ceremony for people who make movies. The television coverage usually begins on the red carpet with interviews and commentary about how each star is dressed and who his or her date is for the evening. Coverage then turns its attention to which celebrities are in attendance and speculation of who will win which award. When the winners are finally announced, they make their way to the podium and accept the Oscar.

It is tradition, at this point, to thank all the people who helped them win. They usually acknowledge friends, family members, managers, and coworkers for making it possible for them to win an Oscar. This is their way of remembering or recognizing that they would never have won without the help of these very important people in their lives.

Read Psalm 105:1–7.

This psalm calls God's people to remember the wonders that He has done. He has done great things for them by delivering them and setting them apart for His glory, and His people are supposed to celebrate and remember all of His goodness. Without the Lord's mighty works on their behalf, they would never have survived.

We must also remember what the Lord has done on our behalf. We should often celebrate and reflect on his great act of redemption for us. Our response to God's grace should be to remember His goodness in redeeming us through the blood of Jesus Christ. Christians should live as thankful, forgiven people who are always remembering and thanking God for the great things that He has done in their lives.

1. LIST SOME OF THE MIGHTY WORKS OF GOD THAT YOU CAN RE-
MEMBER FROM SCRIPTURE.

2. WHAT WONDERS DO YOU REMEMBER THAT GOD HAS WORKED
IN YOUR LIFE?

3. HOW DOES REMEMBERING THE INCREDIBLE WORKS THAT GOD
HAS DONE AFFECT THE WAY THAT YOU THINK ABOUT HIM?

4. WRITE A PRAYER TO GOD BELOW AND THANK HIM FOR ALL OF
THE INCREDIBLE WORKS THAT HE HAS DONE IN SCRIPTURE, IN HIS-
TORY, AND IN YOUR LIFE. COMMIT TO REMEMBERING THE WORKS
OF GOD AND CEASELESSLY CELEBRATING ALL THAT HE HAS DONE.

"I tell you the truth, anyone who will not receive the kingdom of God like a little child will never enter it."

VERSE

nineteen

receive

YOU CAN LEARN A LOT WHEN YOU SPEND TIME WITH CHILDREN. CHILDREN TEACH US HOW TO BE FEARLESS AS THEY EXPLORE THE WORLD AROUND THEM. CHILDREN TEACH US HOW TO LOVE AS THEY GIVE HUGS AND KISSES FREELY. CHILDREN TEACH US ABOUT HAVING FAITH AS THEY BELIEVE COMPLETELY IN THOSE WHOM THEY LOVE AND TRUST.

THESE CHARACTERISTICS ARE BEST SEEN IN RELATIONSHIPS BETWEEN CHILDREN AND THEIR PARENTS OR GUARDIANS. CHILDREN DEPEND ON THEIR CAREGIVERS FROM THE MOMENT THEY ARE BORN. THEY COULD NOT SURVIVE WITHOUT THEM. AS CHILDREN GROW OLDER, THAT TRUST REMAINS AND GROWS, AND THEY RARELY QUESTION THE ABILITY OF THEIR PARENTS TO CARE FOR THEM.

READ MARK 10:13–16.

IN THESE VERSES, WE FIND THE DISCIPLES PUSHING THE CHILDREN AWAY—ONLY TO BE REBUKED BY JESUS FOR DOING SO. JESUS EXPLAINS THAT THESE CHILDREN ARE THE EXAMPLE THAT ALL SHOULD FOLLOW. HE SAID THAT IF WE CANNOT RECEIVE THE LOVE OF GOD AND THE KINGDOM OF HEAVEN IN THE SAME WAY THAT CHILDREN DO, THEN WE WOULD NOT RECEIVE THEM AT ALL.

CHILDREN DO NOTHING TO DESERVE THE LOVE AND PROVISION OF THEIR PARENTS, BUT THEY STILL RECEIVE THEM FREELY. IN THE SAME WAY, WE MUST RECEIVE THE GIFTS OF GOD'S LOVE, REDEMPTION, AND KINGDOM AS CHILDREN DO. THIS PASSAGE PAINTS A BEAUTIFUL PICTURE OF THE GREAT GIFT THAT GOD OFFERS US AS OUR HEAVENLY FATHER. UNFORTUNATELY, SOMEWHERE ALONG THE WAY, WE TURNED FROM CHILDLIKE FAITH AND FOR THE FIRST TIME DID NOT TRUST THAT GOD'S GIFTS ARE GOOD. WE BEGAN TO RELY ON OURSELVES AND SEEK OUR OWN PLANS AND DESIRES. WE EVEN LET OUR EXPERIENCES WITH OUR PARENTS OR GUARDIANS INFLUENCE HOW WE VIEWED GOD. INSTEAD, WE MUST RECEIVE HIM AND HIS KINGDOM WITH OPEN ARMS, JUST LIKE LITTLE CHILDREN.

REDUCE
REGARD
REPLY
REVEAL
REQUEST
REBUKE
REFLECT
RELY
RESCUE
REASON
REBUFF
REMEMBER
REVIVE
REACH
RECEIVE
RESOLVE
RESIGN
RESTORE
RETAIN
REPRESENT
RETREAT
RETURN

1. What are some examples of things in which you trusted completely as a child without question?

2. What do you think that it looks like to accept the Kingdom of God like a child?

3. What barriers exist in your life that keep you from practicing faith like a child?

4. Write a prayer to God below and ask Him to help you learn what it means to have faith like a child. Thank Him for being better than even the best that parents can possibly be. Commit to openly and freely trusting in and relying on Him for your whole life.

> ## Job 22:21
> Submit to God and be at peace with him; in this way prosperity will come to you.

Lordship. It's kind of a funny word, isn't it? Lordship. It evokes thoughts of medieval knights, castles, shields, and swords. The word has ancient roots, but it's still very much in use today. The word "Lord" is used throughout the Bible to refer to God. We also use it in our description of Jesus as our "personal Lord and Savior." But what does it really mean?

Read Job 22:21–28.

The book of Job contains a lot of conversations between Job and his friends in which they try to sort out why bad things keep happening to him and his family. Here, Job's friend Eliphaz tries to convince him that it is his sin that has caused all the trouble in his life. Eliphaz pleads with him to submit to God and be at peace with Him. In Eliphaz's mind, this would end Job's suffering.

In his plea, we see a clear picture of lordship. Lordship means that we give complete control over to someone else. We submit our thoughts, desires, and will to what the Lord knows to be best. We submit to the Lord's plan because we know that it is good and right, even when we cannot see how everything is going to play out. We resign ourselves to following His lead wherever it may take us and at whatever cost. The fruit of this resignation is peace and prosperity that God alone can give.

So what is keeping you from fully resigning your life to God? Why don't you believe that God knows best? Can you think of a time when God's plan didn't turn out to be the best? So why are you doubting Him now? Resign yourself to his lordship, and rest in the peace of the Father who intimately cares for you and has your best interests in mind.

]REFLECT

1. What is your personal definition of the word lordship?

2. In what ways do you currently need to resign to God's leading in your life?

3. What things are preventing you from being fully resigned to God as Lord?

4. Write a prayer to God below and express to Him your desire for Him to be Lord of your life. Confess any hang-ups you have that are currently preventing your full submission. Commit to resigning all illusions of control that you might have and to following His leadership no matter where it takes you.

RESIST

JAMES 4:7

Submit yourselves, then, to God. Resist the devil, and he will flee from you.

TEMPTATION IS A STATE OF BEING THAT EVERY SINGLE ONE OF US KNOWS ALL TOO WELL. WE CAN COMPLETELY RELATE TO WHAT IT FEELS LIKE TO SEE THAT CHOCOLATE CAKE SITTING ON THE COUNTER THAT WE KNOW WE'RE NOT SUPPOSED TO EAT BEFORE DINNER. WE KNOW THE ALLURING DRAW TO POST A CRAZY STATUS UPDATE WHENEVER WE NOTICE THAT OUR FRIEND FORGOT TO SIGN OUT OF THEIR FACEBOOK ACCOUNT. WE'VE EXPERIENCED THE CAPTIVATING TRANCE THAT TAKES HOLD WHEN WE SEE THE ANSWERS FOR NEXT WEEK'S TEST JUST LYING ON OUR TEACHER'S DESK WHEN SHE LEAVES THE ROOM.

IN ANY OF THESE SCENARIOS, AND COUNTLESS OTHERS, WE ARE FACED WITH A CHOICE. DO WE GIVE INTO TEMPTATION'S SEDUCTION AND FULFILL OUR MOST DEPRAVED DESIRES. OR DO WE RESIST. RUN AWAY, FAR AWAY, PUTTING AS GREAT A DISTANCE BETWEEN US AND THE TEMPTATION, SEEKING HELP FROM SOMEONE MUCH STRONGER THAN US THAT CAN ENSURE WE WON'T BE ENSNARED BY TEMPTATION'S TRAPS. UNFORTUNATELY, TOO MANY TIMES WE OPT FOR THE FIRST OPTION, SOMETIMES EVEN THINKING THAT THE SECOND IS JUST TOO HARD.

READ JAMES 4:7-10.

WHEN WE CHOOSE TO LIVE A LIFE IN SERVICE TO GOD, WE IMMEDIATELY BECOME A TARGET OF THOSE FORCES THAT SEEK TO THWART GOD'S WILL IN ANY WAY POSSIBLE. THE DEVIL KNOWS OUR WEAKNESSES AND HOW TO EXPLOIT THEM. HE KNOWS JUST WHAT TEMPTATIONS WILL BE MOST APPEALING TO US AND IS MASTERFUL AT MANIPULATING US INTO THE MOST VULNERABLE POSITION POSSIBLE. WHEN WE CONSIDER THAT THE DEVIL IS WORKING AGAINST US, WE CAN SOMETIMES BE LEFT FEELING LIKE WE DON'T STAND A CHANCE AT ALL.

BUT WE DO. THE DEVIL CAN BE RESISTED. OF COURSE, THIS ISN'T SOMETHING THAT WE'RE EXPECTED TO DO ALL ON OUR OWN. NOR CAN WE. ONLY WHEN WE SUBMIT FIRST TO GOD ARE WE ABLE TO RESIST ANY TEMPTATION.

1. What temptations do you face that you find most alluring?

2. How do you need to be active in resisting these temptations?

3. In what ways does submission to God enable you to resist the devil?

4. Write a prayer to God below expressing your full submission to Him. Share with Him the temptations you're currently facing and ask Him to help you to resist them all.

2 CORINTHIANS 5:20

We are therefore Christ's ambassadors, as though God were making his appeal through us. We implore you on Christ's behalf: Be reconciled to God.

The People to People Ambassador Program is an organization that exists to provide students with the opportunity to travel abroad and demonstrate the belief that every student can make a difference and create peace in the world. Students who are part of this program represent their community, school, state, and country to everyone that they come in contact with during their travels.

Along with the privilege that it is to be selected to be part of one of People to People's journeys, there comes a great responsibility. Many people will form opinions about the U.S. based on how its citizens represent their country.

Read 2 Corinthians 5:17–20.

Here, Paul is writing to the church in Corinth about its members being reconciled to God through Christ. He is saying that because believers are reconciled through Christ, they are therefore to be ambassadors of Christ, representing Him in all that they do. Paul also emphasizes that Christ-followers are to implore, or beg, nonbelievers on Christ's behalf so that all will be reconciled to God.

So what does this mean for you? Well, if you are a Christ-follower, then the message is very clear. You have been saved by Christ and reconciled to God. Therefore you are now an ambassador of Christ. This means that all that you do, say, and think should be done as a representation of Jesus Christ. This can seem like a pretty daunting task because it in fact is. But also recognize what a joy and an honor it is. We sometimes wonder just how God desires to use us in the world. This is the answer: We are meant to represent Him to everyone around us. Could there be anything better?

1. WHAT EXACTLY DO YOU THINK IT MEANS TO REPRESENT JESUS
CHRIST?

2. IN WHAT WAYS DO YOU BELIEVE THAT YOU REPRESENT HIM WELL?

3. IF ALL THAT SOMEONE KNEW ABOUT JESUS WAS GAINED
FROM OBSERVING YOU, WHAT WOULD HE OR SHE THINK ABOUT
HIM?

4. WRITE A PRAYER TO GOD BELOW AND THANK HIM FOR THE GREAT
PRIVILEGE AND RESPONSIBILITY THAT HE HAS GIVEN TO YOU TO
REPRESENT JESUS TO EVERYONE AROUND YOU. CONFESS THE TIMES
WHEN YOU HAVEN'T DONE THIS VERY WELL. ASK FOR HIM TO
CONTINUE TO USE YOU IN GREAT WAYS TO MAKE HIM KNOWN.

*Let us examine our ways and test them, and
let us return to the LORD.*

VERSE

twenty-three
return

MSNBC HAS A SHOW TITLED *LOCKUP* THAT GIVES A BEHIND-THE-SCENES LOOK AT WHAT IT IS LIKE TO BE A CONVICTED CRIMINAL. THE SHOW HELPS ITS VIEWERS VISUALIZE FROM THE SAFETY OF THEIR HOMES WHAT LIFE IS LIKE ON THE INSIDE OF A VERY DANGEROUS PLACE.

HERE'S HOPING THAT YOU'LL NEVER GAIN FIRSTHAND EXPERIENCE AS A PRISONER IN A JAIL—BUT CAN YOU IMAGINE THE HORROR OF LOSING YOUR FREEDOM? EVERY MORNING YOU WAKE UP IN A PRISON CELL WITH ROOMMATES YOU DIDN'T CHOOSE, ONLY TO BE FORCED TO DO WHATEVER SOMEONE ELSE TELLS YOU TO DO. YOU HAVE NO CHOICE ABOUT WHAT YOU EAT, WHERE YOU GO, OR EVEN WHEN YOU SHOWER. THIS WOULD BE A VERY DIFFICULT WAY OF LIFE.

READ LAMENTATIONS 3:39—40.

THOUGH WE PROBABLY DON'T THINK ABOUT IT AS OFTEN AS WE SHOULD, IT IS IMPORTANT FOR US TO RECOGNIZE THAT WHEN WE LIVE IN SIN, WE ARE LIVING IN REBELLION TO GOD. BY BREAKING HIS HOLY LAW, WE ARE LIVING AS CONVICTED CRIMINALS WORTHY OF THE PUNISHMENT OF DEATH. THEREFORE WE MUST RETURN AND FOCUS OUR HEARTS ON THE LORD'S RIGHTEOUS PLAN. CHOOSING SIN OVER OBEDIENCE RESULTS IN A LACK OF FREEDOM BECAUSE SIN ALWAYS HAS CONSEQUENCES. THERE IS NO JOY, NO HOPE, AND NO FREEDOM WHEN WE IMPRISON OURSELVES WITHIN SIN.

THE GOOD NEWS, THOUGH, IS THAT WE SERVE A GOD WHO IS RICH IN MERCY AND LOVE. BECAUSE THIS IS TRUE, WE CAN FREELY CHOOSE TO EXAMINE OUR LIVES AND RETURN TO GOD. DOING SO RESULTS IN PRAISE, GLORY, AND HONOR FOR THE NAME OF THE LORD IN THIS FALLEN WORLD. SO LET US EXAMINE OUR WAYS AND RETURN TO OUR GOD IN ORDER TO TRULY UNDERSTAND WHAT FREEDOM IS. WE WILL FIND THAT HIS WAY IS BETTER AND THAT HIS PURPOSE IS ALWAYS GREATER THAN OUR SIN.

REDUCE
REGARD
REPLY
REVEAL
REQUEST
REBUKE
REFLECT
RELY
RESCUE
REASON
REBUFF
REMEMBER
REVIVE
REACH
RECEIVE
RESOLVE
RESIGN
RESTORE
RETAIN
REPRESENT
RETREAT

1. In what ways have you found yourself to be a prisoner of sin in the past?

2. In what ways might you be a prisoner of sin right now?

3. Describe what it means to return to God.

4. Write a prayer to God below and confess your sins. Ask Him and thank Him for His forgiveness of your sins. Commit to returning to Him, remaining with Him, and seeking after His plans and purposes for your life.

> **Ephesians 1:7**
> In him we have redemption through his blood, the forgiveness of sins,
> in accordance with the riches of God's grace.

Heading into the 2006 Winter Olympics in Torino, Italy, world champion U.S. skier Bode Miller was projected to win multiple medals. But fans watched in disbelief as not only did Miller not win gold in Torino—but he didn't even make the medal stand in any of the five races in which he competed. The reason? Rather than taking advantage of the great athletic gift that he had been given, He instead took it for granted and tried to use it to make his life as easy and pleasurable as possible. As a result, Miller became undisciplined and unprepared and almost quit the sport.

Four years later, at the 2010 Winter Olympics in Vancouver, Canada, a refocused Miller finally won the gold that had eluded him in the last Olympics. In the eyes of many, Miller's Olympic skiing career that had been tainted by his previous failure was finally redeemed.

Read Ephesians 1:3–8

Miller's story of athletic redemption is inspiring, but it's not nearly as inspiring as our story of redemption through Jesus Christ. We were a hopeless people, unable to save ourselves from our sinful nature. But God had special plans for us. He gave his only Son to die on the cross for our transgressions. The wrath that should have been poured out on us was replaced with the blood of Jesus, and we were covered in grace instead.

Because of this blood, forgiveness, and grace, we are now a redeemed people. The penalty for our sinfulness has been paid, bought by the sacrifice of Jesus. We now live in a right relationship with God because we have believed in His sacrifice and committed our lives to Him. There is no other story of redemption that can compete with God's story of love that has been so graciously lavished on us.

⌐REFLECT

1. What do you think it means to be redeemed?

2. How have you experienced redemption in your life?

3. How would you say that the sacrifice of Jesus Christ has redeemed you before God?

4. Write a prayer to God below and thank Him for His grace and mercy. Praise Him for the redemption that He has worked in your life.

PSALM 5:11

But let all who take refuge in you
be glad; let them ever sing for joy.
Spread your protection over them,
that those who love your name may
rejoice in you.

LIFE ISN'T EASY. THAT'S NO BIG NEWS FLASH, BUT IT'S ALSO NOT SOMETHING THAT WE THINK ABOUT VERY MUCH UNLESS WE'RE GOING THROUGH A PARTICULARLY HARD TIME. DURING DIFFICULT PERIODS OF LIFE, WE OFTEN FIND THAT THE ONE THING WE WANT TO DO IS ESCAPE, TO JUST GET AWAY AND REST SOMEWHERE THAT WE KNOW WILL KEEP US SAFE. WE ARE OFTEN NEVER AS THANKFUL AS WHEN WE FINALLY FIND A PLACE LIKE THAT.

READ PSALM 5:1—12.

IN PSALM 5, THE PSALMIST PLEADS WITH GOD TO ENACT VENGEANCE ON HIS ENEMIES. WHILE WE DO NOT KNOW HOW GOD RESPONDED TO THIS REQUEST, WE DO KNOW THAT THE PSALMIST CONCLUDES THIS REQUEST IN VERSE 11 BY DECLARING THAT THE CORRECT RESPONSE FOR ALL WHO TAKE REFUGE IN GOD IS TO REJOICE. THE PSALMIST GOES ON TO SAY THAT THOSE WHO TAKE REFUGE IN GOD SHOULD SING FOR JOY, LOVE HIS NAME, AND REJOICE IN HIM. THE PICTURE THAT WE ARE GIVEN IS ONE OF WORSHIP. EVEN WHEN THE WORLD IS OUT TO GET US, WE CAN TRUST GOD FOR DELIVERANCE AND PROTECTION. WHEN WE TRUST HIM AND EXPERIENCE HIS FAITHFULNESS TO WATCH OVER US, WE SHOULDN'T FORGET TO LET HIM KNOW JUST HOW GRATEFUL WE ARE.

OUR RESPONSE TO THIS GREAT GOD SHOULD BE GREAT WORSHIP. WE SHOULD DECLARE THAT GOD IS HIGH AND WORTHY OF OUR DEVOTION AND ALLEGIANCE. WE SHOULD REJOICE IN THE FACT THAT WE HAVE A GOD WHO LOVES AND CARES INTIMATELY FOR US AS HIS CHILDREN. WE SHOULD REJOICE IN HIS REFUGE AND THAT HE SENT HIS ONLY SON JESUS TO TAKE ON THE PENALTY FOR OUR SINS BECAUSE HE LOVES US. CONSIDER THE PLACE OF REFUGE THAT GOD HAS BEEN FOR YOU—AND DON'T NEGLECT TO REJOICE IN HIM FOR ALL THAT HE HAS DONE IN PROTECTING YOU AND FOR HOW FAITHFUL AND TRUSTWORTHY HE CONTINUES TO PROVE TO BE.

1. *Describe a time in your life when you wanted to escape and take refuge somewhere.*

2. *In what ways has God been a refuge for you in the past?*

3. *In what ways do you need God to be a refuge for you now?*

4. *Write a prayer to God below and thank Him for being a trustworthy place of refuge from the struggles of this world. Focus your prayer on worshiping Him for all that He has done. Close by asking Him to shelter and protect you from whatever current struggles you are facing.*

PROVERBS 15:23

A man finds joy in giving an apt reply; and how good is a timely word!

Have you ever found yourself at a complete loss for words in a situation only to finally think of exactly what you should have said hours or even days later after it's too late? Maybe someone was making fun of your friend and you really wanted to put them in their place but kept coming up blank. Perhaps that certain someone you've been crushing on finally talks to you in the hall, but instead of being super-smooth, you look like a moron when you can't seem to put a sentence together.

The usual problem in these types of circumstances is being caught completely off guard. You're just so unprepared for what's happening around you that it's like your brain isn't able to fully process it. You don't end up just saying the wrong thing. You're unable to come up with any reply at all. But then there are those situations where your wit is quick and you immediately know the exact right thing to say. In those moments, it seems that nothing feels better. You're on top of the world and nothing can bring you down.

Read Proverbs 15:23.

Isn't it amazing when you discover something in God's Word to which you can completely relate? It's obvious here that the writer of this proverb knew precisely how good it feels to know the right thing to say at the very right time. The question, though, is how can we prepare ourselves to be able to do that more often. Well, in order to say the right thing you have to know what is the right thing to say. To put it more simply, in order to reply with God's Word you have to know God's Word. That's it, and there's nothing better when you do.

1. DESCRIBE A SITUATION IN WHICH YOU WISHED YOU COULD HAVE THOUGHT OF THE RIGHT THING TO SAY.

2. WHY DOES IT FEEL SO GOOD TO SAY THE EXACT RIGHT THING IN THE EXACT RIGHT MOMENT AND SITUATION?

3. HOW DOES KNOWLEDGE OF GOD'S WORD AFFECT OUR ABILITY TO REPLY WITH IT WHEN WE NEED TO?

4. WRITE A PRAYER TO GOD BELOW THANKING HIM FOR HIS WORD. ASK HIM TO HELP YOU GROW IN YOUR KNOWLEDGE OF SCRIPTURE AND TO HELP YOU BE PREPARED TO GIVE AN APT REPLY IN ANY SITUATION.

"So I say to you: Ask and it will be given to you; seek and you will find; knock and the door will be opened to you."

VERSE

request

ALLOW ME TO NOW INTRODUCE YOU TO MAUREEN. MAUREEN IS 24-YEARS-OLD, LIVES IN NAIROBI, KENYA, AND GREW UP IN ONE OF THE MOST DANGEROUS SLUMS IN ALL OF AFRICA. AS A CHILD, SHE BEGGED TO BE BROUGHT OUT OF POVERTY. SHE WANTED TO LIVE SOMEWHERE SAFE, SOMEWHERE SHE COULD SLEEP IN PEACE AT NIGHT, AND SOMEWHERE SHE WAS GUARANTEED FOOD AT LEAST ONCE A DAY.

WHEN MAUREEN FIRST HEARD OF JESUS CHRIST, SHE SPENT HOURS A DAY PRAYING TO HIM, ASKING HIM TO RELEASE HER FROM POVERTY. IT DIDN'T HAPPEN, AND SHE DIDN'T UNDERSTAND WHY. WHEN ASKED TO EXPRESS WHAT SHE FELT ABOUT POVERTY, HER CONSTANT RESPONSE WAS THAT SHE HATED IT, THAT IT WAS UNFAIR, AND THAT HER LIFE WAS AWFUL BECAUSE OF IT. FOR YEARS SHE MADE HER REQUEST KNOWN TO GOD TO FREE HER FROM THESE CONDITIONS, AND FOR YEARS HER REQUEST SEEMINGLY WENT UNANSWERED.

READ LUKE 11:1–12.

THE THEME HERE IS PRAYER. VERSES 9–10 ARE FAMILIAR TO MANY OF US, BUT THEY CAN BE VERY CONFUSING AS WELL. DO THESE VERSES REALLY MEAN THAT WE'LL RECEIVE WHATEVER WE ASK OF GOD? NOT EXACTLY. WE SHOULD HUMBLY MAKE REQUESTS OF GOD REGARDING THE NEEDS OF OTHERS AND OURSELVES. WE SHOULD ALSO FERVENTLY PURSUE HOW IT IS THAT GOD DESIRES TO RESPOND TO OUR REQUESTS. WHEN WE PRAY, WE ARE TO BE PERSISTENT AND CONFIDENT THAT GOD KNOWS WHAT IS BEST FOR US AND WILL PROVIDE EXACTLY THAT. THAT'S WHAT IT MEANS TO ASK, SEEK AND KNOCK.

TODAY, WHEN ASKED WHAT SHE THINKS ABOUT POVERTY, MAUREEN SAYS, "I THANK GOD FOR POVERTY. WITHOUT IT, I WOULD HAVE NEVER SURRENDERED MY LIFE TO CHRIST JESUS AND FOUND HOPE IN HIM, MY LORD AND SAVIOR." THE WAYS THAT OUR PRAYERS ARE ANSWERED MAY NOT ALWAYS LOOK EXACTLY LIKE WHAT WE WANT, BUT THEY WILL ALWAYS BE WHAT GOD HAS IN MIND.

REDUCE
REGARD
REPLY
REVEAL
REQUEST
REBUKE
REFLECT
RELY
RESCUE
REASON
REBUFF
REMEMBER
REVIVE
REACH
RECEIVE
RESOLVE
RESIGN
RESTORE
RETAIN
REPRESENT
RETREAT
RETURN

1. What are some things for which you are currently praying?

2. How would you like for God to answer these prayers?

3. How does trying to seek what God wants affect the way that you pray?

4. Write a prayer to God below and present to Him any requests that you might have. Tell Him the answers to these requests that you want. Commit, however, to ultimately seeking His answers above yours—and seeking until you have His answers.

---

2 Corinthians 3:18
And we, who with unveiled faces all reflect the Lord's glory, are being transformed into his likeness with ever-increasing glory, which comes from the Lord, who is the Spirit.

Weddings are one of the most significant and sacred ceremonies that the Church recognizes today. In addition to being a religious ceremony, a wedding is also a time of great celebration. At most weddings, the groom and bride gather their families and friends together for a weekend and essentially throw a party to celebrate their union as husband and wife.

One thing in particular that you (especially you ladies) probably notice at a wedding is how beautifully the bride is dressed. As the doors to the sanctuary swing open, she walks in wearing a gorgeous white dress, which is sure to attract the attention of everyone in the room. Her face is usually covered with a veil for a symbolic reason. Traditionally, the father of the bride lifts the veil so that her face is revealed to the groom first. This represents the transfer of care from the father to the groom. This is recognition of a love relationship that starts the process of growing more intimate over many years to come.

Read 2 Corinthians 3:12–18.

We now have access to the Lord through Christ and His Spirit that lives inside of us. Through this relationship we reflect the glory of God and become more like Him by walking with Him daily. When we turn to Christ, the veil is lifted so that we can know God. This is the beginning of the love relationship that Christians share with God. It is in this moment that believers begin a lifelong process of becoming more like Him.

Just as the groom is able to see his bride in all her beauty when her veil is lifted, we now see God because of the lifting of the veil from over our hearts. This results in praise, glory, and honor to Jesus Christ, the one doing the revealing and the one being revealed.

]REFLECT

1. What is in your life that sometimes makes it difficult to understand God?

_____

_____

2. In what ways does the Spirit work to lift this veil from your life?

_____

_____

3. How do you currently reflect the Lord's glory to the world around you?

_____

_____

4. Write a prayer below to God and ask Him to continue helping you to understand Him and grow in Him. Thank Him for continuing to transform you more and more into His Son's likeness.

JEREMIAH 22:3

"This is what the LORD says: Do what is just and right. Rescue from the hand of his oppressor the one who has been robbed. Do no wrong or violence to the alien, the fatherless or the widow, and do not shed innocent blood in this place."

ON JANUARY 12, 2010, A DEVASTATING EARTHQUAKE HIT THE COUNTRY OF HAITI. THE EARTHQUAKE DESTROYED HOMES AND BUILDINGS AND LEFT COUNTLESS PEOPLE TRAPPED, SERIOUSLY INJURED, OR DEAD. PEOPLE FROM ALL OVER THE WORLD RESPONDED TO THE DISASTER. DOCTORS, NURSES, AND RESCUE WORKERS TRAVELED TO THE RAVAGED COUNTRY TO HELP IN WHATEVER CAPACITY THEY COULD.

ALONG WITH THE RESPONDERS COMING TO HAITI, THERE WERE THOSE WHO WERE ALREADY IN HAITI AND WHO REFUSED TO LEAVE. TWO SUCH PEOPLE, A COUPLE, HAD BEEN LIVING IN THE COUNTRY OF HAITI LONG BEFORE THE EARTHQUAKE HIT. THEY HAD UPROOTED THEIR LIVES IN THE UNITED STATES TO BECOME MISSIONARIES AND OPERATE AN ORPHANAGE IN THE PORT-AU-PRINCE AREA. IN THE DAYS FOLLOWING THE EARTHQUAKE, THEY TIRELESSLY SOUGHT WAYS TO SERVE THE HURTING IN THE COUNTRY THAT THEY WERE BURDENED TO LOVE. THEY EVEN TURNED THEIR ORPHANAGE AND HOME INTO A MAKESHIFT HOSPITAL AND TREATMENT CENTER. THEY WERE THE PERSONIFICATION OF HOPE, RELIEF, AND RESCUE TO THE PEOPLE IN THE MIDST OF TRAGEDY.

READ JEREMIAH 22:2–5.

THE MISSIONARY COUPLE IN HAITI PROVIDES US WITH A GOOD EXAMPLE OF WHAT THE LORD IS REQUIRING OF US IN THESE VERSES. HERE, JEREMIAH PAINTS A PICTURE OF THE RESPONSIBILITIES OF AN IDEAL KING AS HE PROPHESIES ABOUT WHAT JESUS WILL DO IN HIS MINISTRY IN THE WORLD.

JESUS DEMONSTRATED IN HIS MINISTRY THAT THE CHRISTIAN FAITH IS NOT INTENDED TO BE A PASSIVE ONE. RATHER, GOD DESIRES FOR US TO BE ACTIVE IN HIS MISSION. PART OF THAT MISSION INCLUDES SEEKING JUSTICE AND HELPING THOSE WHO HAVE BEEN WRONGED OR STRUCK BY TRAGEDY. WE ARE TO BE THE IMAGE OF CHRIST TO THOSE WHO ARE HURTING AND IN NEED. SO SEEK OUT THOSE WHO ARE IN NEED. FIND WAYS TO FREE THOSE WHO ARE OPPRESSED. BECAUSE YOU ARE A FOLLOWER OF CHRIST, THIS IS A CALL THAT CANNOT BE IGNORED.

1. *Whom do you know is struggling with a tragedy?*

2. *In what ways can you be involved in helping to "rescue" that person from his or her suffering?*

3. *Who has helped rescue you in the past whenever you were the one suffering?*

4. *Write a prayer to God below and thank Him for being the ultimate source of rescue in our lives. Commit to answering His call to join Him in rescuing the afflicted and oppressed in the world. Ask Him to help you make the most of every opportunity that you have to join Him in this work.*

ISAIAH 57:15

For this is what the high and lofty One says, he who lives forever, whose name is holy:
"I live in a high and holy place, but also with him who is contrite and lowly in spirit, to
revive the spirit of the lowly and to revive the heart of the contrite."

Have you ever been part of a long-distance relationship? Maybe you have a friend who moved far away or a family member who lives in a different time zone. Regardless of the specifics, the bottom line is that there is this person who means a great deal to you—but you often feel very disconnected from him or her because of the great distance between the two of you. It's hard for those relationships to feel close emotionally when the people involved are so far apart geographically, isn't it?

Have you ever felt that way about your relationship with God? Have you ever felt that, try as you might, you just could not genuinely worship Him, and so you wondered if He even understood what was going on in your life? Maybe right now you're involved in a struggle or have done something that you think is so bad that you're convinced that He's totally abandoned you.

Read Isaiah 57:14–19.

For a while, Isaiah speaks out against the Israelites for worshiping idols instead of God. But about halfway through the chapter, Isaiah changes tracks and starts talking about how God will revive and restore those who are low in spirit and sorry for turning away from Him.

For those of us who feel distant from God, we need to be reminded that He has promised to come and dwell with us. His rightful dwelling is in a high and holy place, but He also promised to dwell with and revive us if we turn to Him and are sorry for sinning against Him. God will stoop down and dwell with us and breathe new life and peace into us. He promised to restore our hearts and give life back to our spirits. So turn to Him. Turn from your sins and run to Him. Open yourself up and allow Him to revive your spirit and heart.

1. WHEN HAVE YOU TRIED TO MAINTAIN SOME KIND OF LONG-DISTANCE RELATIONSHIP WITH SOMEONE?

2. DESCRIBE A TIME IN YOUR LIFE WHEN YOU FELT DISTANT FROM GOD.

3. HOW DOES YOUR PERSPECTIVE ON THINGS CHANGE WHEN YOU REALIZE THAT GOD HAS PROMISED TO DWELL WITH US AT OUR LOWEST MOMENTS AND REVIVE OUR LIVES?

4. WRITE A PRAYER TO GOD BELOW TO THANK HIM FOR DWELLING WITH THE LOWLY AND FOR SEEKING TO REVIVE THE LIVES OF THOSE WHO CALL UPON HIM. CONFESS YOUR SINS AND COMMIT TO TURNING TO GOD AND SEEKING AFTER A DWELLING WITH HIM.

But those who hope in the LORD will renew their strength.
They will soar on wings like eagles; they will run and not
grow weary, they will walk and not be faint.

VERSE

thirty-one
renew

YOU'RE PROBABLY AWARE OF THIS ALREADY, BUT THERE
ARE ACTUALLY PEOPLE WHO LIKE TO RUN. THEY CHOOSE
TO DO IT BECAUSE THEY THINK IT'S FUN. MAYBE YOU'RE
ONE OF THOSE PEOPLE. IF YOU ARE, I WANT YOU TO KNOW
THAT THE REST OF US THINK YOU MIGHT BE A LITTLE CRA-
ZY. WE SEE NO APPEAL IN RUNNING AND THINK THAT THE
ONLY REASON IN THE WORLD WE COULD HAVE FOR POS-
SIBLY DOING IT IS IF SOMEONE IS LITERALLY CHASING US
AND THREATENING BODILY HARM. FOR WHATEVER REA-
SON, WHEN THE REST OF US TRY TO RUN, THE EXPERIENCE
WE HAVE WOULD BE DESCRIBED AS ANYTHING BUT FUN.

HOWEVER, I'M GOING TO LET YOU IN ON A LITTLE SECRET.
HERE IT IS. A LOT OF US NON-RUNNERS REALLY WISH WE
WERE RUNNERS. THAT'S RIGHT. IT'S TRUE. WE WANT TO BE
IN SHAPE. WE WANT TO BE ATHLETIC. WE WANT TO HAVE
AN EXCUSE TO ENJOY THE OUTDOORS WHILE LISTENING TO
OUR IPOD. WE WANT OTHER NON-RUNNERS TO BE ENVIOUS
OF US AND WONDER HOW IN THE WORLD WE WERE ABLE TO
MAKE THE TRANSITION.

THE PROBLEM IS THAT WHEN WE GIVE IT A SHOT, WE JUST
GET WORN OUT SO QUICKLY, USUALLY ABOUT THE TIME
WE HIT A HILL. WHAT WOULD BE PERFECT IS IF WE COULD
SOMEHOW TRADE WITH YOU, IF WE COULD HAVE YOUR
STRENGTH AND YOUR ABILITY TO HELP US GET THROUGH
THOSE HARD CLIMBS.

READ ISAIAH 40:29-31.

NEWS FLASH: LIFE'S HARD. EVEN THE CHRISTIAN LIFE
IS HARD, ESPECIALLY THE CHRISTIAN LIFE. WE CAN GET
WORN DOWN PRETTY QUICKLY AND FAIRLY EASILY. WHAT
WE NEED WHEN WE DO IS TO HAVE OUR STRENGTH RE-
NEWED, TO BE ABLE TO EXCHANGE IT OUT FOR ANOTHER.
THAT'S JUST WHAT GOD ENABLES US TO DO. HE RENEWS
OUR STRENGTH WITH HIS, AND THAT'S A GOOD TRADE.

REDUCE
REGARD
REPLY
REVEAL
REQUEST
REBUKE
REFLECT
RELY
RESCUE
REASON
REBUFF
REMEMBER
REVIVE
REACH
RECEIVE
RESOLVE
RESIGN
RESTORE
RETAIN
REPRESENT
RETREAT
RETURN

1. What situations in life are you currently facing that are wearing you down?

2. How do you feel when life has you completely worn out?

3. What difference does it make to know that God promises to renew your strength with His?

4. Write a prayer to God below admitting how worn down you currently are. Confess the hope that you have in Him and seek His renewal of your strength. Commit to continue on with Him.

CLOSING

Well, you've reached the end (good job, by the way). I hope that in the time you've spent with God's Word that you've been refreshed, renewed and rejuvenated. I pray that you've been able to relate with God in a very real way and have responded to all that He has revealed to you.

If nothing else, I want you to know how proud I am that you spent time retreating from the demands of the world in order to find how rewarding it can be to simply rest in God. I rejoice with you for the work God has done in your life and want to challenge you to remember and reflect on all that you have realized as a result of your time with Him. Though you're finished with this book, the effects of how God has used it in your life will continue to remain. As you journey on, let me offer a few suggestions of things I'd like you to resolve to do.

First, repeatedly study Scripture. I'll be the first to tell you that any enlightenment you've gained from your time with this book has nothing to do with the words we wrote. It is the power of God's Word working in you. Continue spending time with the Word. There are other books like this one that can help you do so, as well as great study Bibles and other resources that will assist you in growing more and more in your knowledge and understanding of God and the Bible.

Second, rely on the Holy Spirit. He is with you. He empowers you. He helps you and guides you and teaches you. He won't fail you.

Third, relate with one another. You're not the only one learning how to reflect God's character in response to His faithfulness. There are many, many others. Get together with some fellow Christ-followers on a regular basis. Encourage one another. Support one another. Pray for one another. Hold each other accountable. Do God's work together.

Thanks again for reading.

regulars

THIS BOOK WAS TRULY A COLLABORATIVE EFFORT; A HANDFUL OF WRIT-
ERS AND ARTISTS CHIPPED IN, EACH BRINGING THEIR OWN UNIQUE PER-
SONALITIES AND CREATIVE VOICES. THIS WAS A GREAT EXAMPLE OF LIFE
AS THE PEOPLE OF GOD, SERVING TOGETHER AS A UNIFIED COMMUNITY.
EVEN THOUGH WE'RE ALL A LITTLE DIFFERENT, WE ALL FOLLOW THE SAME
SAVIOR, PRAISE THE SAME GOD, AND TRUST THE SAME SCRIPTURE INSPIRED
BY THE SAME SPIRIT. WE HOPE YOU HAVE GROWN IN YOUR RELATIONSHIP
WITH CHRIST AND HAD AS MUCH FUN READING THESE DEVOTIONALS AS WE
DID PRODUCING THEM.

AUTHORS
Brad Barnett
Laurabeth Barnett
Beth Ann Hill
Graham Hill
Chris Kinsley

EXECUTIVE EDITOR
Chris Kinsley

COPY EDITOR
Jason Odom

GRAPHIC DESIGN
Katie Beth Shirley

ART DIRECTOR
Drew Francis

PUBLISHING ASSISTANTS
Lee Moore
Janie Walters